Detroit:

Workers, Teachers, Lovers

poems by

William T. Langford IV

Finishing Line Press
Georgetown, Kentucky

Detroit:

Workers, Teachers, Lovers

Copyright © 2022 by William T. Langford IV
ISBN 978-1-64662-856-8 First Edition
All rights reserved under International and Pan-American Copyright Conventions. No part of this book may be reproduced in any manner whatsoever without written permission from the publisher, except in the case of brief quotations embodied in critical articles and reviews.

ACKNOWLEDGMENTS

I extend my heartfelt gratitude to the editors of the publications and organizers of the competitions in which these poems, or versions of these poems first appeared:

Publications
"Shop Around," *Broadside Lotus Press*
"Recipe for a Coney Dog," *East Lansing Art Festival Poetry Press*
"Schooled" & "Uncommon Will," *Michigan State University*
"Saturday, Detroit Eastern Market," *2 Bridges Review*
"Detroit: Exodus," *Belt Publishing*
"Nocturne "*Culture Cult Magazine & Press*

Anthology
"Avatars," *Civilization in Crisis*

Competitions/Awards
"Shop Around," Motown Museum: Motown Mic Spoken Word Artist of the Year
"Schooled," American Advertising Awards Best In Show

Publisher: Leah Huete de Maines
Editor: Christen Kincaid
Front Cover Art: "Will The Poet: Lake Malawi (Day)" 9x13 Mixed Media on Canvas by William T. Langford IV
Rear Cover Art: "Will The Poet: Lake Malawi (Night)" 9x13 Mixed Media on Canvas by William T. Langford IV
Front Cover Text Art: Isabella Kercorian
Author Photo: Dr. Rachel Laws Myers

Order online: www.finishinglinepress.com
also available on amazon.com

Author inquiries and mail orders:
Finishing Line Press
PO Box 1626
Georgetown, Kentucky 40324
USA

Table of Contents

Dear City 1

Nightshift 2

Morning Weather with Sonny Elliot 3

While Listening to Dave Brubeck's "Take Five" 5

Land Bank 6

Saturday, Detroit Eastern Market 8

Schooled 10

Uncommon Will 13

Spirits of Detroit 17

Dig 18

Avatars 20

Round Trip 22

Making a Coney Dog, Detroit Style 23

I Remember You Told Me 24

Shop Around 26

Crew 29

Reasons to Love My Father 31

Detroit: Exodus 32

Biography 34

For my Mother, my first and best teacher

For my Father, the hardest working man I've ever known

For Detroit

For my Love

Dear City

For the Phillip Morris smog
the cigarette-tinged night sky that it will not turn loose
and from this valley, these mountains, I cannot breathe you deeply,
can't brace my falls against your stump,
your roots, deep and distant.

We are reminded by the moniker our city will never shake: Motown.
We are reminded by the earthy howl of dust and glass, winding
through (the long abandoned) Central Station.

We must, but no longer are steel, City.
Can no longer bear, from this particular womb,
such rugged fruit to feed our children.

Dear City,
I long for the sprawl
of your interstate,
green bridges' steel ribcages,
expanding
with the breath
of graffiti,
sprawling, like
exodus.

Oh steel city,
scraping Canada with your untamed borders,
how I steal you in my dress: the twist of my cap—
Honolulu blue lion
roaring from its brim—
with the sticker affixed.

Oh steel city,
oil slick,
slipping
from me.
City I left.
Oh steel city.

Nightshift

Rise,
night-cogs,
integral to our
day-walker slumber,
chasing the fleeing things,
prettying the dirty things.

Rise,
watchmen,
wading into diners,
clocking into quarry,
changing post at door-side.

Though the tile floor will always be stained
with daytime grime and trampled gum,
though no one's entered that door
in days, weeks, turning to ages,
though the fleeing things will
take flight into the crevices,
though the pretty things
will be dirtied,
you will rise
and shine
Again.

Morning Weather with Sonny Elliot

My father drove a black utility truck,
emblazoned with a highlighter-yellow stencil,
"Detroit Board of Education,"
spray painted on both sides.
He'd sit me on his broad lap,
the truck's panel doors peeled back
so we could feel the Michigan air kiss
our faces and hands.

We'd listen
to the throaty purr—
somewhere between a smoker's cough
and the rumble of gym shoes
tumbling alone in a dryer—
of the 6 liter, 200 horsepower
diesel engine
spitting exhaust
into the morning.

My father's head,
dapper in its trademark
Kangol cap,
nodding knowingly
as he trafficked the radio's dial
through waves
of static
to our station.

We'd listen
to AM radio,
W-W-Jayyyy...News Radio Nine Fif-tyyyy,
my father humming,
me, belting out the jingle,

my father's lips
drawn up and back
toward his worker's jaw
into a worker's smile.

Detroit's favorite weatherman
might have called for snow that day,
snow that'd make stepping outside
as comfortable
as sleeping
on a bed of saltine crackers!
We knew when to pause
for Sonny's one-liners.
My father and I learned his rhythm together;
the first poetry I can remember.

We've done alright for ourselves, son,
my father might say,
I, his tiny foreman,
with the air
of a builder
laying down his hammer
for the day,
though his work had only begun.

While Listening to Dave Brubeck's "Take Five"

At day's end,

I said don't swing no more.
I said, Dad, don't swing no more.
Working man, lay down your hammer

at day's end.

Rest, jazz man—
improvising dinner for four boys and wife.
Rest, jazz man, *Take Five*

at day's end.

Your forearms are heavy,
the blacktop tar of the roof boils, sun-hot,
the planks and shingles weigh like steel beams on your back

at day's end.

Working man, lay down your hammer.
It has paid for every road trip and Christmas gift.
I said don't swing no more, Dad, don't swing no more

at day's end.

Lie in the bed you made with that hammer,
under the roof you keep up.
You own this shade

at day's end.

Your walk is a shuffle.
I see the reddened whites of your eyes
and the weary blues of your shoulders' wide arch

at day's end.

I said don't swing no more.
I said, Dad, don't swing no more.

Land Bank

This single-family fixer-upper
is priced to *move*.
Give it a few coats of eggshell—
no, seashell—
you know what?
Let's go with some nice artificial siding,
there's just no hiding the way
a few decades
of housing discrimination
can ruin a perfectly good coat of paint.

You know what?
What say we
scrap my finders-fee?
While the crenellated moldings
are the original mahogany,
unfortunately,
the community
that gave this neighborhood its
je ne sais quoi
is *not* included in this listing.

For full disclosure:

We're currently unable to provide
your family
with Black grannies
in silk hats stacked with flowers.
As such,

the delegation will not be available
to empower your testimonial
of urban renewal
with the requisite *amen*.

No Rolls Royce Phantom
will escort a teenager in a pink tuxedo
and black Jordans to the prom.

This is a *peaceful* community.

No booms, and absolutely
no baps
will wake you from your beauty winks.

No complicated daps
with palms
slapping together
like thunderclaps
will be exchanged
on your street corner.

No inexplicable shirtless man on horseback,
no creamsicle Camaro,
no ice cream truck
bumping trap music through metal bullhorns
will parade on *your* block.
Don't you worry.

In that moment
after the streetlights
click
on
you will not be disturbed by the cheers
of buzzer beaters
drained as the shot clock expires!
or last touchdowns scored
or the cacophony of mothers
Pied Piper-ing their children home for the night.

None of that.

What you're buying here isn't a house.
It is an investment
in the future of this city,
a home,
someplace
quiet.

Saturday, Detroit Eastern Market

*Our Father who art in heaven,
hallowed be thy name.*

Thy kingdom come
with red brick arches,
translucent plexi-glass doors, agape,
meat and sweet shops,
ample parking for the caravans.

Thy kingdom come,
with mango, supple melon for the yuppies,
fairly-priced unsold cobs of corn for the Desert Storm Vets,
Vietnam Vets on active duty—the forage for fortune,
palms upturned to judgment:

Yeah buddy, everybody's got a story.

They write like music, in movements:
Military crawl,
some in chairs, some with bottles—
through the urbangrowth,
insulate their jackets with pages
from free hymnal books
dispensed like soups and rations.

Give us this day the gospel growl of your fruit mongers,
with their shout-worn pipes warm,
vibrating with their earth-dust-coated palm creases.

Give us this day
the chorus of backup-beeping semis,
their eighteen wheel-rolling steel bodies
with their ware-hauling hollows, brimming.

Give us this day
the murmuration of mothers making mental math,
their brow-furrowing effort to piece meals
with their dollars, WIC, cents.

Give us this day
the cacophony of children's growling bellies,
their gang-fight-rumbling insides
with their imploring eyes:

Give us this day
our daily bread,
as it is
in heaven.

Schooled

One minute
I was poet at Detroit's Cass Tech High.

The next
a reality check,
I was a Spartan, marching
amongst the thousands.

I bet you've felt it. . .
on a Tuesday,
between organic chemistry
and lunch in the Union,
it hits you:

*You're from another time zone,
and you're the only one like you.*
Tucked in the palm of the mitten,
you can't see yourself fitting in here:

Frigid winter white outs,
Go Green! Go White! shout outs,
you've got your campus map out. . .

the midnight scream in finals week,
all this
at the expense of your beauty sleep.

Back home,
maybe they
Roll Tide
or the Friday night lights
shine on games of cricket.

Maybe
there's a sea breeze and salt smell,
not these
salted sidewalks
chalked and graffiti-stenciled.

You penciled in
a chat with your mother
which begat the fear that you're out of your depth
which begat something nasty
deep in your chest...

You can expel it.
You are wanted here.
You are different.

These chains are
begging to be broken.

We're choking on the
dust of indifference
but we're spitting back
our insistence that
coexistence is not enough.

These chains' nagging links
are begging to be broken
by the sun rising on the day
when I'm not taken
to be a token
excepting the fact that I do
stand for change,

choking
on the glass, class, and status
at the back of my throat,

I do stand for change.
It's rolling along the banks of this red cedar.

I see it there in *you*
hunched over a book,
sprinting headlong on the track,
headstrong in a lecture,
waist deep in a conjecture,

that expects that we'll connect
with respect
for the reality that we are
vastly different
like magma and mercury
rising to the occasion
to celebrate what makes us
if only in a nod
or smile say,

You're welcome here

Poet,
preacher, teacher,
reacher out,
salsa dancer,
free lancer,
deep in your books
le gourmet cooks...

It's all here,
under this sun.
This son yearns for it
because a dream lives here,
in our sparks and our kindling.
We have only to let it burn.

Uncommon Will

Somewhere,
a call echoes,
and ears are closed
to girls with
gigabytes in their veins,
and minds for rockets and fractions,
subtracted from
the math of inclusion in science.

The call says, "Who will?"
Who hears of these trials?

Somewhere
a freshman—
the first generation to go to college—
seeks not veneration,
just to be acknowledged
among so many,
by someone.

Who will?
Spartans Will

beseech a student to see that he is indispensable, individual, and yet part
of a team.

We're a patchwork tapestry
bursting at its seams
with stories, histories, languages, and creeds.
We're forming ranks of weavers,
the makers of dreams.

On the banks of the Red Cedar,
there's a school that's known to all.
Its reach spans the whole globe,
and we do more than play good ball.

We're questing for solutions
to the pressing quandaries of our age
searching and researching

to bring forth
a luminous future
gauged

by cleaner
power
and streams
of pristine aqua

that feed fields
that feed families
that feed change
you can count on.

We're leaders
and we're stout,
we're fighters,
and we're outstretched in
arms
to welcome you
to our global home,

because you're always in Spartan Nation,
no matter where you roam.

You'll find us,
marching forth
into the good
and uncertain
in union
unearthing
possibility
from scant chance
and philosophy from stone.

We're seeders of knowledge crops
tilling the earth for fertile loam.

This
is the dreamwork

of divergent minds
in concert:

We're meeting "impossible"
with defiance,
reliance on this Spartan phalanx,
our ranks
hundreds of thousands strong,
our legacy,
suited for poets' song,
sings of

psychoacoustics,
reading the music of the brain
sings in string quartets,
trembling hands
shaking your soul with vibrato, bravado,

sings of
the sweet string music
of 6 Final Fours,

sings of imaginations
shorn of their moorings

sings of
teachers
stretching minds
like power lines,
to push against
and break
the brink
of ordinary.

And our impact
can't be packed and shipped
and moved by freight;
it's not bought and sold
and loaded in crates.

It's not in a crest,
laden with gold and old age.

It's weighed
in scores of lives
and the possibility to change
for the better
just one,
and another,
and another...

Who Will?
Spartans Will.

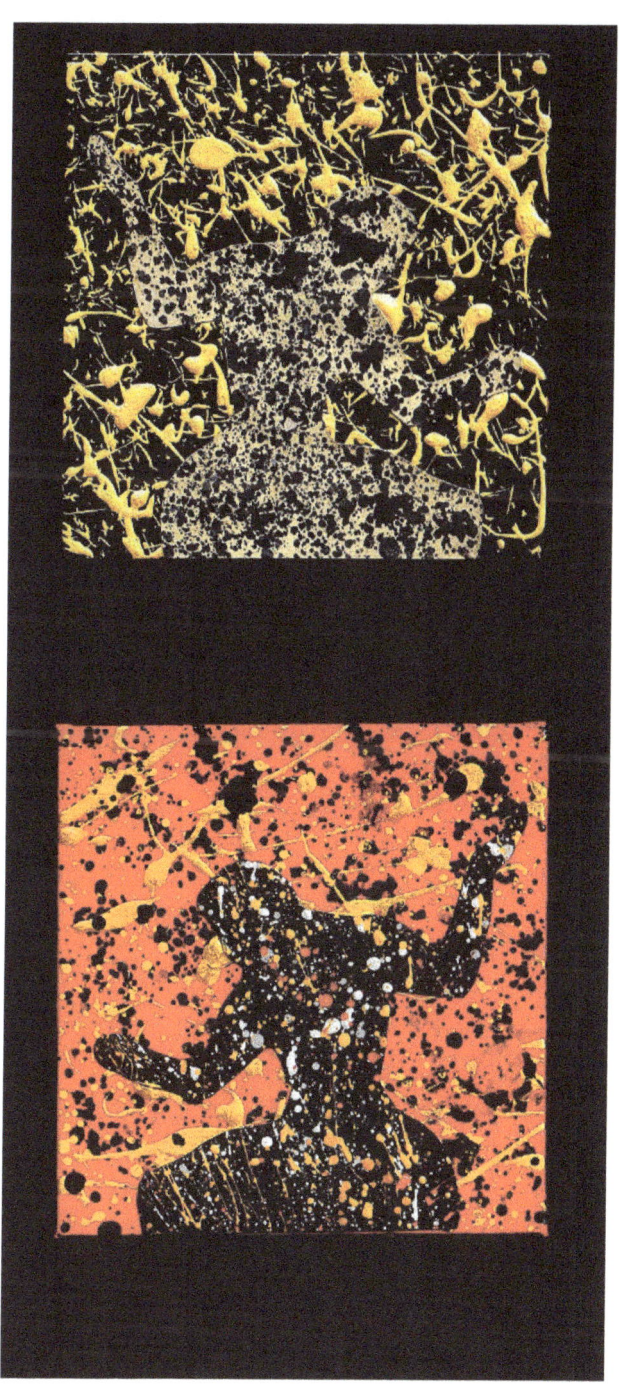

"Spirits of Detroit" (Series)
Canvas Paintings By William T. Langford IV

Dig

Perhaps your grandfather was a revolutionary
I know so little of your past
Perhaps it is sewn into a mismatched
patchwork quilt in Promise Land Tennessee
or etched onto your skin
into your calloused palms
like chocolate crop circles

Either way
as your heir, I
weave your past incessantly
I'm fabricating something so grand

Father
let me sing to you the tale
of your great-great grandmother
an orator to rival the eloquence of
Emerson, of Moriarty
who lamented two-fifths of every black man lost to ignorance

There are no records
there are merely photographs
graying into obscurity
of men in borrowed suits
who must be our genesis, father

Their shoulders are wide, father
like yours
like mine

Look at that posture
the sin of pride in something
straightening their backs

There are no librarians to send searching
no historians to send hunting
no archaeologists to send digging

For what has been buried
For lack of a scribe
by the passage of time
in my flesh

Send no men, father
bespectacled, and curiosity peaked
khaki-clad, and shovel ready
in search of what I am
what we are

We will tell our story
I at the loom
today

Avatars

We've made it!

The future
weighed us
and found us packing
love for our earth, its oceans
its asylum seekers
its meek and many weary,
found us making music
in the waking hours of tragedy
forging art in back alleys,
making amends
for amendments late to the docket.

Congratulations.

We're notorious for missing the forest for the trees.

It is now your mission to ensure that we
don't miss the road for the digital milestones,
miss the movement
for the buckshot of tweets, scattering matter

when what matters is a smattering of facts,
splattered roughshod over one-hundred and forty characters.

It verges on haiku:
the art of saying so much
and so little,
so briefly.

It is your sacred duty to ensure that
we never forget the moment
smartphones took the place of lighters
at concerts where the bass was especially heavy.

Make sure our next generation of iterations
remembers the time
when the word of mouth

was the word
and the word was good.

I read that the volume of data on Wikipedia alone
cannot be housed by any library
of sensible size.

A veritable Alexandria
stretches before our fingertips
and yawns at our inability to contain it.

I implore you
to contain it,
to write the word
or speak it
to not wait
on change
but to be it,
to be more
than avatars.

Round Trip

I've walked under a lot of lights
that have *spontaneously* deluminated.

But I'd like to believe:

> that you won't
> cut the lights off on me,
> as I'm climbing the basement staircase
> of the hard days
>
> that you won't stop looking for the good in me,
> the God in us,
> the odd in me.
>
> I'd like to believe
> that you see me,
> my shadow elongating
> in that glow of yours,
>
> that you'll stop
> ponder
> if I would stumble,
> unsure without the torch of you
>
> to light the dark steps
> for my footfalls.

Making a Coney Dog, Detroit Style

Naturally, you'll use all-beef hotdogs,
Koegel brand, so perfectly pink and plump.

Fresh is a must, but any bun will do
to swaddle this Detroit delicacy.

Layer on *beanless* chili (a service
to us all), with bumpy bits of spiced beef.

Top with yellow onion's ghost white insides,
granules strewn like salt on an icy walk.

Add a single stripe of yellow mustard
for the purists; ketchup for the tourists.

Nest in a hinged white clamshell container
for the greasy take-out jewel inside.

Of course, you'll need a strong-stomached people.
Find them waiting tables, schooling children.

I Remember You Told Me

That you couldn't give blood
because your heart was beating too fast
and the nurse said *no*

I don't want to write another love poem
lest the people grow weary of this—
the prose of the throes of us

But maybe just this once
more
once more

Once
born into this world was a woman
Play-Dough-shaped
to fill
the space in the pit of me

Plato scaped
our world in mathematics
to divide us by common factors
now we
mass manufacture love
mass manufacture love

Ptolemy sketched the stars
for the pair of us
Ours was a passion-perilous
flight risk
on nights brisk
when my fingers twitched
to hold your hand

Now I do

Swing low
Sweet cherry ought to be your name
and not for fruit of your harvest
but for the hardness
of your bark

a cedar village
harnessed
to raise the hairs on any man who dreamed to pick you prematurely

in your tall pauses
I beseech you to speak
over my radiator
into my ear
and say it low
if it is not some god I hear
in your voice
then he never reigned

I remember you told me
that you couldn't give blood
because your heart was beating too fast

If your veins need another course
to course through
of course
I'll be your vessel, heart
Especially when the pressure
gets to you
or gets you to Jonesing

for me to write you another poem
and I will
just this once
more
once
more

Shop Around

I can't help myself,
I'm that stubborn kinda fellow
when I'm alone I cry.
I heard it through the grapevine,
What's going on?
Trouble, man.

Mary Wells
is "shopping around for that Motown sound
and so do we Marvelette the news on our doorsteps:
that Detroit is *finally* on the rise,
some Ford Falcon on cinder blocks,
climbing through the ashes
of the ghetto,
a resurrection of our catalogue of woes,
a rose-gold recollection of our greatest hits.

The saints and the spinners would have you believe our hope died in the riots,
the contours of our Bing Steel body
misaligned by the fires,
by the blight.

The temptation's to say
Detroit sees new light
in the Q-line,
in suburban flight
directly into our core,
but you cannot remix and
you cannot
remaster
Cass Corridor with erasure.

This rare earth cannot be so easily purchased
FedEx'd, signed, sealed, delivered
to your doorstep.

They forget
we got that soul clap in our bones
we got that Church-On-Every-Block
Jesus.

Please, Mr. Postman,
deliver us some truth.

Tell 'em 'bout Black Bottom:
how we bounce back from devastation
like dandelions,
gnarled and still shinin,'
Joe Louis on the ropes,
gliding through shots to the body.

THIS is the Motown Sound
a supreme, three-part Copacabana cornucopia
to uncloud your cornea and
God is writing this album
from the top down.
We're living for the city,
we're headed for higher ground.

I've watched Detroit,
thought drowned,
thought derelict,
thought defunct,
rise
like the Earl of Funk.

Through our intellect,
the eyes see, brothers,
the miracles on every corner:

Detroiters, hustlin' harder,
from the Check 'N' Go
on Campau,
to the wonder of young Stevie
sound checking the Apollo.

From bowls of beans
to Beans Bowles
fingertips building an Empire
on the Boulevard,

so my lady
can go dancing
in the streets,
can click her heels
three times in a warehouse

brimming
with enough mortar
to brick back every barbershop,
every black business cropped
in the reaping,

so we can stand in the shadows of Motown,
in the footsteps
of Martin, marching down Woodward
undeterred,
toward
something that feels like our dream
undeferred,
and bathe in the cool
of Hughes.

My lady no longer
sings the blues,
she is as fond as ever of your mahogany
Detroit
is the sound of young America
hungry and full
and hungry and full
of music
like tides
the push and pull
of our penance

like
tithes cast upon the plate glisten
if you would but lend your ear
to listen.

Crew

For Hilary and Dan

Here, we find the fruition
of a love that sings from Billy's Strings
to the shores of Charlevoix.

A love that
knows the meaning of intuition:

that the two of us
could remix any disaster
together.

When we run this gauntlet,
my Definite,
there's simply no
whether or not.

Be the rapids grand
or the distance long,
let the waves break
Maui-strong
against the rocks
and we'll be boulders
holding steadfast against the deep.

My rock rolls with me
when the toll
is especially vast.

If the waters
cannot be contained
by some levee,
you are my ballast.

If a bevy should
break against our bow,
I will *gladly*
take to the sea with you.

From shore
to further shore,
of us
I'm sure, Love.

Be it a pagoda
in Kyoto
a log cabin in Tahoe,
I'll go with you,
to Traverse the City
neon lights bright
on our faces...
or count the paces
to the tree line
on our farm,
the lifelines of our palms

say
*Pack lightly
and disregard the weather
Wherever we are to go
let us go,
Together.*

Watch a Audio/Video Performance of "Crew"

Scan Here

Reasons to Love My Father

Because you call me 'Bill the Thrill,'
eat habanera peanuts,
always manage to rub your eyes.
Because you make the best omelets
with green pepper,
red onion,
mozzarella cheese and
honey-glazed ham.

I needed to escape

but stayed
for the pauses in your morning phone calls.
Because you take the biggest bites of my sandwiches.
Because you won the nail-driving contest
against men
half
your age.

Despite late arrivals.
Because you've spilled coffee on every surface in the car.
Because you eat the sugar-free ice cream
for diabetics.

Because you cut the backs from your brown Cole Haans
to make flip-flops.

Because your laugh is rare.
We bear the same stitched scar
on different arms.

Detroit: Exodus

It is heavy, heavy, reeeal heavy
and we're back brother
like barbershop crisp high-top fades
and kicks
in the barbed bosom
of the city that harbored us
hardened us
and made us shine
with smoke on its skyline
tectonic plate-like shifting pavement
and steel in its breath

We're on the I-75
I'm shotgun in your Chevy
It is heavy, heavy, *reeeal* heavy
We're back brother
Like Bob Marley's "Exodus" is on wax
and spinning in reverse
calling us home
home
is where my heart is buried in a tar

It is heavy, heavy, *reeeal* heavy
like oil sands
sweat glands pouring crude
these rude boys
and American girls
dolls, addie-kink curls
locked,
cocked back and loaded
goaded into entering the
inviting night of
my city's rumbling belly

It is heavy, heavy, reeeal heavy
with Coney dogs
and strip malls
We're back for both
back from both coasts
with pea coats and stubble
and it's different

we're older
from here, of here
Detroit bred here
and fed here
but left here. . .

We're part of a generation
that must take flight
to fight our Reputation

We *are* the Exodus,
Yes
and we will be the Genesis
of a Detroit built of books
and the bright crooked tooth smiles
of children whose bright future will be no myth, brother
Our evolution will be live and televised for those eyes cast askance
live and televised for the fair-weather fans
our winters are too harsh for you

It is cold in the D
and we're tucked deep Southeast in the mitten
It is fitting then
that you fear what it is we do in the dark
Hark, my burning lover calls my name

So sip your wine, tourists
Enjoy your casinos
We've gone,
but we'll be back
You've spent just enough time gambling
to know you should *always* bet on black

William T. Langford IV
Biography

William T. Langford IV, AKA Will "The Poet" Langford, is a community-engaged teaching artist and Fulbright ETA Alumnus (Kenya). He divides his energy between education and community development projects in Michigan, the U.S, and in East Africa, alongside the Children & Youth Empowerment Center in Nyeri, Kenya. Will is also a visual artist—drawing inspiration from Detroit's vibrant community of mural artists.

Langford's poetry is focused on themes of resilience, hard work, and unity. As a teenager growing up on Detroit's west side, Langford's English teacher gave him a copy of Claude McKay's "If We Must Die." It was then that Langford knew that poetry could do so much more than rhyme: it could be a revolution unto itself, it could have teeth, it could transport him anywhere.

Will Langford is the 2017 Motown Mic Spoken Word Artist of the Year. As a performance artist, Langford's poetry has garnered "Best of Show" in the American Advertising Awards, a Michigan Emmy Award, and the 2021 Mark Ritzenhein Emerging Poet Award, sponsored by the Lansing Poetry Club.

Langford's art has appeared in or is forthcoming from: *The Detroit Neighborhood Guidebook, Ilanot Review, Work/6, Falling Hard, 2 Bridges Review*, and Finishing Line Press.

You can learn more about Will "The Poet" Langford at www.WillThePoet.Com and keep up with his community engagement work on Instagram: @WTLThePoet

Scan To Visit www.WillThePoet.com

www.ingramcontent.com/pod-product-compliance
Lightning Source LLC
Chambersburg PA
CBHW050821090426
42737CB00022B/3468